The Big Book of Bible Facts

Rhona Pipe

Illustrated by
Graham Round

HUNT&
THORPE

Copyright © 1996 Hunt and Thorpe
Text © 1993 by Rhona Pipe
Illustrations © 1992 by Graham Round

ISBN 1 85608 279 2

Originally published 1993

In Australia this book is published by:
Hunt & Thorpe Australia Pty Ltd.
9 Euston Street, Rydalmere NSW 2116

The Bible version used in this publication is THE NEW KING JAMES VERSION. Copyright © 1979, 1980, 1982, Thomas Nelson, Inc., Publishers.

A CIP catalogue record for this book is available from the British Library.

Manufactured in Hong Kong.

CONTENTS

1 FACTS ABOUT THE BIBLE

1 Book that isn't a book

The word *Bible* comes from a Greek word. *Biblia* means "books." Picking up a Bible is like picking up a stack of books. In fact, there are 66 books. It is sort of like picking up a library. And there are more than 35 authors. There are a king and a tax collector, a doctor and a shepherd.

4 Longest chapter

The longest chapter is Psalm 119. It has 176 verses. The psalm is divided into 22 sections. Each section has 8 verses. Every verse in the first section starts with the first letter of the Hebrew alphabet. Every verse in the second section starts with the second letter of the alphabet. Every verse in the third section begins with the third letter. This goes on through the whole psalm. All 22 letters of the Hebrew alphabet are used.

2 Total number of words in the Bible

In the Bible there are about 773,692 words. That equals about 3,566,480 letters. It would take you 70 hours to read the whole Bible aloud.

3 Shortest verse

Each book in the Bible is broken into chapters. Each chapter is broken into short sections. The sections are called verses. All of the verses are numbered. So it is easy to find your way around. The shortest verse is John 11:35. It says, "Jesus wept."

5 Middle verses

Open the Bible halfway through. You will hit the book of Psalms. The middle verses of the Bible are verses 1 and 2 of Psalm 117.

6 Longest book

The book of Psalms is Israel's hymnbook. It contains 150 hymns and prayers. It's the longest book in the Bible.

7 Shortest book

Jesus' friend John wrote three letters in the New Testament. One of them, 2 John, has only 13 verses. That makes it the shortest book in the Bible.

8 Bible languages

The Old Testament was written in Hebrew. The New Testament was written in Greek. The Bible has now been translated into many languages. It can be read in nearly half of the 5,445 languages of the world.

9 What the Bible looked like

The Ten Commandments were written on slabs of stone. Later, the books of the Bible were written on flat strips of papyrus. They were made from papyrus reeds that grew by the Nile. The sheets of papyrus were fastened together. Then they were rolled up into long rolls or scrolls.

10 Beginning with a chisel

Long ago, when people wanted to write something, they used a chisel on rock. Sometimes they used a stylus on clay. It was easier to go from right to left for most people. So Hebrew writing goes from right to left. The first page of the Hebrew Bible is the *last* page. Short notes, like shopping lists, were written on broken bits of pottery!

2 DISCOVERIES ABOUT THE BIBLE

1 One of the oldest cities

On the site of ancient Jericho is a round stone tower. It was built over 7,000 years ago. It was built in the New Stone Age. This was before the pyramids were built. A spring of water and an oasis made Jericho a welcome sight for travelers. It was known as "the city of palm trees."
(See Deuteronomy 34:3.)

2 Oldest piece of the New Testament

Archaeologists dug up some ruins in ancient Egypt. They found a piece of papyrus with part of John 18 on it. Someone had copied it about 100 years after Jesus died.

3 King Solomon's walls

The king of Egypt burned Gezer down. Then Solomon ordered it to be rebuilt, along with Hazor and Megiddo. The walls and gates of the towns are almost the same. This shows that Solomon's builders used the same master plan.
(See 1 Kings 9:15-17.)

4 King Hezekiah's secret tunnel

A boy discovered Hezekiah's Tunnel. He accidentally fell into the Pool of Siloam. In the rock, he saw a small hole. It led to a narrow passage. The passage turned out to be a secret tunnel. King Hezekiah built it 700 years before Jesus' birth. It linked the people of Jerusalem to their only water supply. It saved their lives when Jerusalem was besieged.
(See 2 Chronicles 32:30.)

7 Clay proof

The Bible says that King Cyrus of Persia let all his Jewish captives go back to Jerusalem. Hard to believe? Historians thought so. Then they found the clay Cyrus Cylinder. The records on it tell how Cyrus released all captive peoples. He also gave them money to restore their temples.
(See Ezra 1:1-4; 6:3-5.)

8 Black stone of Moab

Mesha was the king of Moab. He erected the Moabite Stone in about 840 B.C. It celebrated his success in war against Israel. The writing on the stone is about YHWH. That is the special name given to God in the Bible.
(See 2 Kings 3:4-5.)

5 Shepherd boy's discovery

A shepherd boy stumbled across some very old clay pots in a cave by the Dead Sea. Inside, he found only dusty old scrolls. He was disappointed. He had wanted gold. But the scrolls were worth more than gold. They were ancient copies of the Old Testament. They were hundreds of years older than any other copies in the world. They prove that the Old Testament we have today has not changed since it was first written down.

6 Stargazing

The Star of Bethlehem was not just reported by Matthew. About the time of Jesus' birth, Chinese astronomers recorded it, too. For a short time they saw in the skies a bright, unknown star. Astronomers now think the star the wise men saw could have been a supernova.

3 THE LAND

1 Lowest sea

The Dead Sea is the lowest sea in the world. It is 1,300 feet below sea level. Where it is deepest, it is 1,300 more feet below sea level. No water flows out of it. Its salts and minerals kill all fish and plants. The Old Testament writers call it the Salt Sea.
(See Genesis 14:3.)

2 Sea Jesus preached from

The Sea of Galilee is also known as the Sea of Tiberias (see John 6:1) or the Lake of Gennesaret (see Luke 5:1). It is about 12 miles long and 7 miles wide. It has many fish. It is known for its sudden strong storms. Many people crowded around Jesus. So He sat in a boat while the people stood on the shore. "Then He spoke many things to them in parables." (See Matthew 13:2-3.)

3 Famous Bible desert

Many events in the Bible took place in one area. This land is between Persia in the east and Egypt in the west. Much of the land is desert, like the Arabian desert and the Syrian desert. The Israelites wandered for 40 years in the desert lands between Egypt and Israel. They did not trust God enough to enter the promised land.

4 Minerals and metals of the Bible

In King Solomon's day the copper mines near the Gulf of Aqaba were a busy place. The Philistines knew how to smelt iron ore into metal. Later the Israelites learned the skill in David's time. In Deuteronomy 8:9, God promised Israel "a land whose stones are iron and out of whose hills you can dig copper." Other metals named in the Bible are gold, silver, lead, and tin. The Bible also names the minerals brimstone, flint, niter, and salt.

5 Water from a rock

The Israelites had no water to drink as they went through the desert of Sin. They complained to Moses. Moses asked the Lord what he should do. The Lord told Moses to "strike the rock, and water will come out of it, that the people may drink."
(See Exodus 17:6.)

6 Famous Bible mountains

Many important events in the Bible took place on mountains. Jesus was transfigured on a mountain. He also went up to heaven from a mountain. The Old Testament tells about three men who met with God on the tops of mountains: Abraham on a mountain in Moriah (see Genesis 22:2-14); Moses on Sinai (see Exodus 19:20–20:21); Elijah on Mount Carmel (see 1 Kings 18:16-46).

8 Where Jesus grew up

We know little about Jesus' boyhood. But we do know something about Galilee, where he grew up. Galilee was well-known for its fishing industry and its farming. A number of trade routes crossed through Galilee. It was a center for trade. Many of the events in the Gospels took place in Galilee.
(See Luke 4:14-16, 31-37.)

7 Israel's longest river

Israel's longest river is the river Jordan. The Bible talks often about the Jordan. It rises close to Mount Hermon in the north and flows into the Sea of Galilee. Then it flows on through the Jordan Valley and into the Dead Sea. Many Bible events center on the river Jordan.
(See Joshua 3:1-17; 2 Kings 5:1-14.)

9 Bible's most famous valley

The Jordan Valley is part of a famous geological rift known as the Great Rift Valley. This stretches from Syria in the north, through the Red Sea, and down into central Africa. The Jordan Valley, or Jordan Rift, forms the lowest place on the earth's surface. Many Bible events happen in the Jordan Valley. One such event is Jesus' baptism in the river Jordan.
(See Matthew 3:1-17.)

4 OLD TESTAMENT BOOKS

1 **Shortest Old Testament book**

The shortest Old Testament book is the prophecy of Obadiah. It has one chapter with 21 verses. It predicts God's judgment on the evil people of Edom. (See Obadiah 10.)

2 **Shortest verse in the Old Testament**

The Old Testament is full of family trees. The shortest verse in the Old Testament comes in the middle of one of these. It is in the thirteenth Old Testament book, 1 Chronicles. Verse 1:25 has 3 names, just 12 total letters: "Eber, Peleg, Reu."

3 **Oldest parable**

The oldest parable in the Bible is in the book of Judges. In it, some trees try to persuade an olive tree, a fig tree, a grapevine, and a thornbush to be their king. (See Judges 9:8-15.)

5 **Grandfather of the Reformation**

People have called the writer of the short Old Testament prophecy of Habakkuk the grandfather of the Reformation. He wrote this famous verse: "The just shall live by his faith." The apostle Paul learned justification by faith from this passage. The leading Reformer Martin Luther learned it from Paul. (See Habakkuk 2:4; Romans 1:17; Galatians 3:11.)

4 **Old Testament references to Jesus Christ**

There are more than 60 Old Testament prophecies about Jesus. These were fulfilled hundreds of years later – during His lifetime. Micah 5:2 prophesied the place of Jesus' birth. It was fulfilled in Matthew 2:6: "But you, Bethlehem … out of you shall come forth to Me the One to be Ruler in Israel." Psalm 22:18 says, "They divide My garments among them, and for My clothing they cast lots." Matthew tells of this happening at the foot of Jesus' cross in Matthew 27:35.

6 Humor from Proverbs

Proverbs is packed with wise sayings and helpful moral advice. It contains a number of funny passages. How about these descriptions of a careless woman and a lazy man? "As a ring of gold in a swine's snout, so is a lovely woman who lacks discretion." "As a door turns on its hinges, so does the lazy man on his bed." (See Proverbs 11:22; 26:14.)

7 Old Testament book quoted most often in the New Testament

The New Testament contains more than 260 Old Testament quotations. About 90 quotations come from the first 5 books of the Bible. Around 50 quotations come from the prophecy of Isaiah. And 30 quotations are from the Minor Prophets. But the Old Testament book quoted most often is Psalms. The New Testament quotes Psalms more than 70 times.

8 Old Testament book that doesn't mention God

The book of Esther never talks about God. This Old Testament book is set in the time of the Jewish exile in Persia. The Jews were saved from being killed by the courage of Queen Esther. It's not difficult to see God's caring hand behind these events. (See Esther 8:1-8.)

9 Old Testament predictions about the Messiah

The Old Testament contains hundreds of predictions about the coming of a spiritual savior for the Jews and for the whole world. Isaiah 53:5 contains one well-known prediction: "He was wounded for our transgressions." The sufferings of this Messiah are spoken about in many Psalms, such as Psalms 22; 31; 67; 80; and 102.

10 Jesus' love of the Old Testament

Jesus quoted from 19 Old Testament books. He referred to 20 people from the Old Testament. For example, Jesus quotes from the book of Deuteronomy three times in Matthew 4:1-11. One of Jesus' last sayings from the cross – "My God, My God, why have You forsaken Me?" – was from Psalm 22:1. (See Deuteronomy 8:3; 6:16; 6:13; Matthew 27:46.)

5 NEW TESTAMENT BOOKS

1 Shortest New Testament book

We find the shortest book in the New Testament, 2 John, near the end of the Bible. It is the second of John's three letters. It has just 13 verses. Verse 6 is probably the most well-known: "This is the commandment, that ... you should walk in [love]."

2 Longest New Testament book

The longest New Testament book is Acts. It has 28 chapters. Matthew also has 28 chapters. But it is shorter than Acts.

3 Number of verses in the New Testament

The New Testament has 7,959 verses. The 27 New Testament books make up 260 chapters. They are just over one-fourth the length of the Old Testament. One New Testament verse tells the purpose of the Bible. Second Timothy 3:15 says, "The Holy Scriptures ... are able to make you wise for salvation through faith which is in Christ Jesus."

5 Book by a doctor

You would expect a rabbi like Paul to be a New Testament writer. But what about a tax collector (Matthew) and two fishermen (John and Peter)? The person who wrote more of the New Testament than anyone else is a doctor. Luke wrote the gospel of Luke and Acts. (See Colossians 4:14.)

4 New Testament book with most quotations from the Old Testament

The Old Testament was Jesus' Bible. The eight writers of the New Testament all knew the Old Testament well. Mark has 33 quotations from the Old Testament. Luke and John tie with 40 quotations each. But the New Testament book with the most Old Testament quotations is Matthew. It has 70.

6 Longest genealogy

Family trees were important in Bible times. Matthew opens his gospel with the genealogy (family tree) of Jesus. It goes back as far as Abraham. But Luke's version of Jesus' family tree is much longer. It traces Jesus' family back to Adam.
(See Matthew 1:1-16; Luke 3:23-38.)

7 Four portraits of Jesus

Jesus never wrote a book about Himself. Matthew, Mark, Luke, and John didn't write four life stories of Jesus. But each did give a different picture of Him. Matthew links Jesus to the Old Testament. Mark sees Him as the redeemer of all. Luke shows Jesus as the Son of Man. And John tells us why he wrote his gospel: "That you may believe that Jesus is the Christ."
(See John 20:30-31.)

8 Letters from prison

John Bunyan wrote his famous book *Pilgrim's Progress* from a prison in Bedford. The apostle Paul wrote some of his New Testament letters from prison too. There are four "Prison Letters" written by Paul.
(See Ephesians 3:1; Philippians 1:7; Colossians 4:3; Philemon.)

9 Personal letter

Of the 27 New Testament books, 21 are letters. But there is only one personal letter among the 21. That is the short letter from Paul to Philemon. In it Paul pleads for Philemon to take back his runaway slave. "Receive him as you would me," writes Paul in verse 17.

10 Book about the end of the world

The last book of the Bible is the book of Revelation. It is about the last days before Jesus Christ returns to this earth. Persecuted Christians find comfort in it. They see that even evil times in history are not out of God's control.

6 DATES

1 Date of creation

The first verse of the Bible says, "In the beginning God created the heavens and the earth." Bible scholars have tried to figure out this date – with no success. The Bible does not tell us the date of creation, just who the Creator is. (See Genesis 1:1.)

2 Bible's first recorded date

Genesis 5:3 gives us the first date named in the Bible. "Adam lived one hundred and thirty years, and begot a son." People have used this to try to fix an exact date for Adam's life. But the writers of Old Testament family trees sometimes left people out on purpose. This genealogy in Genesis links earliest humankind to the Flood. It was never meant to be an exact time chart.

3 Day the ark came to rest

Genesis 8:4 says: "The ark rested in the seventh month, the seventeenth day of the month, on the mountains of Ararat." No one has found the ark on the Ararat mountain range. That's not surprising. It happened very long ago. "The seventh month, the seventeenth day" shows that the ark's voyage was a real event in history.

4 When Abraham lived

Bible scholars think they know when Abraham lived. He is the first person in the Bible they can know this about. Even here they are not too sure. Abraham was the first of the patriarchs, and he is dated around 2000–1825 B.C.

5 Year the Jews were exiled

We really do know the date of the Jewish exile. The Jews who lived in the kingdom of Judah had their capital, Jerusalem, captured in 587 B.C. Some scholars say that Jerusalem was captured in 586 B.C.!

6 Return of the exiles

Jeremiah prophesied to the people of Jerusalem that they would be defeated. You can guess how popular he was! He was called a traitor. But Jeremiah also said that the Jews would return from exile 70 years later. His prediction was right. The book of Ezra tells about the exile. It begins like this: "Now in the first year of Cyrus king of Persia, that the word of the LORD by the mouth of Jeremiah might be fulfilled …"
(See also Jeremiah 25:11-12.)

8 Birth of Jesus

Now you would think this was the easiest event in the world to date. It must be A.D. 0, or 0 B.C. But, no, it was not! It was around 7 B.C. Why? Jesus was born before the death of Herod the Great. From history we know that this means Jesus was born no later than 4 B.C. (See Matthew 2:1; Luke 1:5.)

7 Destruction of New Testament Jerusalem

People looked with wonder at Herod's beautiful temple in Jerusalem. But Jesus said that "not one stone shall be left here upon another." This prediction came true in A.D. 70. Jerusalem was destroyed then. (See Matthew 24:2.)

9 Worst day in history

The worst day in history was the day the Romans killed Jesus Christ. They used the most agonizing death penalty ever – crucifixion. This happened in A.D. 33. It brought God's forgiveness to us. So the day is not called Bad Friday but Good Friday.

10 Date of the end of the world

We have another unknown date – the date of the end of the world. People have tried all sorts of arithmetic to predict its date. Everyone is wrong! Jesus said that even He did not know it.
(See Matthew 24:36.)

7 TRIBES AND PEOPLES

1 Hebrews
Abraham is the first person in the Bible to be called a Hebrew. Abraham's sons, grandsons, and great-grandsons were also given this name. Today we think of the Jews as the Hebrews to whom God showed His love. (See Genesis 14:13.)

2 People of the pyramids
The pharaohs ruled Egypt for 3,000 years. They built the pyramids. The history of Egypt is broken into the Old Kingdom, the Middle Kingdom, the New Kingdom, and the Decline. Joseph was sold into Egypt as a slave. He became prime minister during the time of the Middle Kingdom.

3 People of the land of milk and honey
Long before Moses became the leader of the Israelites, the Lord God promised him, "So I have come down to deliver them out of the hand of the Egyptians, and to bring them up from that land to a good and large land, to a land flowing with milk and honey, to the place of the Canaanites and the Hittites and the Amorites and the Perizzites and the Hivites and the Jebusites." (See Exodus 3:8.)

5 Assyrians
In the 9th, 8th, and 7th centuries before Jesus Christ, the world power in Bible lands was Assyria. The Jews hated this godless nation. For this reason, Jonah at first refused to obey God when He told Jonah to preach to them in Nineveh. Nineveh was their second largest town. (See Jonah 1:1-3.)

4 Sea people
The Philistines were known as the sea people. They lived on the Mediterranean coast just southwest of the land of Israel. Their most famous champion was the giant Goliath. He was killed by David. (See 1 Samuel 17.)

6 Babylonians

The Jews came up against these powerful people in 587 B.C. The Babylonians destroyed Jerusalem and sent many Jews to Babylon.

7 People of Persia

As the Babylonians grew weak, the Persians took over. They captured Babylonia in 539 B.C. The Bible books of Ezra, Nehemiah, and Esther are set in this time. Cyrus, king of Persia, was a fair ruler. He allowed the Jews to return to their homeland of Judah.
(See Ezra 1:1-11.)

8 Noble Greeks

The influence of the golden age of the Greeks is still with us. We still study philosophers such as Socrates and Plato. Their ideas about government are found in all democratic governments today. Paul preached in the Greek town of Athens with all its idols. And the New Testament was first written in Greek.

9 All-powerful Romans

In Jesus' day the Romans, with their many soldiers, were the world power. The spread of Christianity was helped by the Roman empire. Their famous roads allowed people to travel easily. Their strong armies gave a time of peace. Pontius Pilate was the Roman governor (procurator) of Judea. He gave his permission for the Jews to pass the death sentence on Jesus.
(See Matthew 27:11-26.)

10 First mention of Christians

The word *Christian* started as a nickname for an early follower of Jesus Christ. Acts 11:26 says, "The disciples were first called Christians in Antioch." The word *Christian* or *Christians* is found in only two other places in the Bible: Acts 26:28 and 1 Peter 4:16.

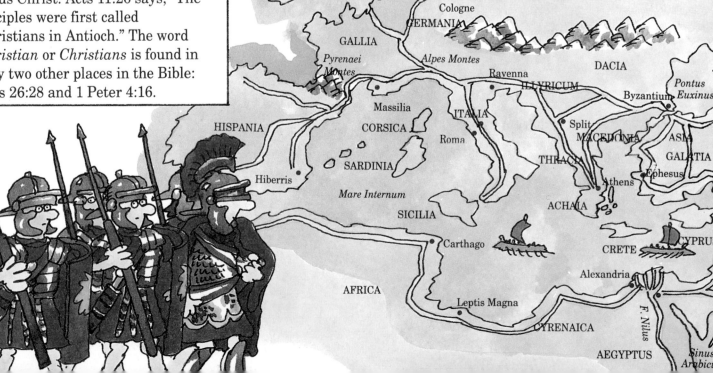

8 OLD TESTAMENT MEN

1 Oldest
Methuselah is by far the oldest person in the Bible. Genesis 5:27 says he died at the ripe old age of 969.

3 Two men who never died
Yes, two men in the Bible never died. Both their names begin with the letter *E*. There was Enoch: "Enoch walked with God; and he was not, for God took him." Then there was Elijah: "Elijah went up by a whirlwind into heaven." (See Genesis 5:24; 2 Kings 2:11.)

2 Fattest
Eglon was king of Moab. He defeated the Israelites and held them down for 18 years. He was very big. When Ehud, a Benjamite, murdered him by sticking a sword into his stomach, the fat closed over it. Ehud shut and locked the doors of Eglon's room. Then he quietly went away. (See Judges 3:12-30.)

4 Goatskin disguise
One man followed his mother's advice. He put goatskins on his hands and part of his neck. In this way smooth-skinned Jacob tricked his dad into giving him the blessing that had been saved for his hairy elder brother Esau. (See Genesis 27:1-40.)

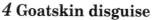

5 Gideon and the sheep's fleece
Gideon, one of the Old Testament judges, wanted God to tell him that he would save Israel. To find out, Gideon put a fleece outside overnight. If there was dew on the fleece but not on the ground, the answer was yes. Gideon got his answer. But he still was not sure. He then asked for dew to be on the ground but not on the fleece. This happened too. (See Judges 6:36-40.)

6 Head and shoulders above the rest

Kish had a son named Saul (1 Samuel 9:1-2). He was the finest young man among the Israelites. He was a head taller than anyone else. But Saul ended up being like a dwarf in his heart. He turned away from God.

7 Kingmaker

Samuel was quite a man. He was a priest and a prophet. He was also a kingmaker. He secretly anointed Saul to be king of Israel when Saul was a nobody. Samuel did the same for David later on.
(See 1 Samuel 9:15–10:8; 16:13.)

8 Shepherd, poet, and musician turned king

King David was one of the most talented men in the Bible. He was a superstrong shepherd. He killed a lion with his bare hands. He composed music and wrote poems (73 of our Psalms bear his name). He killed a giant (remember Goliath). And he was Israel's most successful king. God remembered him because he was a man after God's own heart.
(See 1 Samuel 17.)

9 Head caught in a tree

Absalom ended up with three spears in his heart (2 Samuel 18). He could not defend himself. Verse 9 explains: "Absalom rode on a mule. The mule went under the thick boughs of a great terebinth tree, and his head caught in the terebinth; so he was left hanging between heaven and earth. And the mule which was under him went on."

10 Prophet and his talking donkey

One man learned a lot about God's will from his talking donkey. The prophet Balaam beat his donkey three times for stopping. After the third time, the donkey spoke to him! Then Balaam saw an angel with a sword in the way. So he turned back to doing what God told him to do.
(See Numbers 22:21-41.)

9 OLD TESTAMENT WOMEN

1 Rahab

The Israelites wanted to enter the promised land. They sent two spies to Jericho. Rahab saved their lives by hiding them in some flax. In return for this, Rahab was saved when Joshua destroyed Jericho. She and her family were rescued from her house. A red cord hanging from the window was a sign for the spies.
(See Joshua 2:1-21; 6:17-25.)

2 Woman who laughed at God

Whoever heard of ninety-year-old women having children? When God told Abraham that Sarah was going to have a baby, Sarah laughed to herself. But God replied, "Is anything too hard for the LORD?" And, sure enough, the next year baby Isaac arrived.
(See Genesis 18:10-15.)

3 Female judge

In dark days, Deborah, a prophetess, brought light and hope. The Israelites took their problems to her for help. She also encouraged Barak to lead the Israelite army against Israel's enemies.
(See Judges 4–5.)

4 Woman who cared for her mother-in-law

Ruth had every reason to be bitter. Her husband had died and left her childless. Her mother-in-law, Naomi, was no better off. Naomi's husband and two sons had died. She decided to return to her own land. Ruth went with her mother-in-law. She found food for them both and really cared for her. She married again. King David and, later, Jesus came from her family.
(See the book of Ruth.)

5 Woman whose oil and flour never ran out

The widow at Zarephath was about to prepare the last meal for her son and herself. Her food was about to run out. What a time for Elijah to ask for a small cake of bread! He then told her that her oil and flour would last through the famine. She never ran out!
(See 1 Kings 17:7-16.)

6 Woman mistaken for someone who was drunk

Hannah felt the biggest sadness possible for a Jewish married woman. She was childless. At Shiloh she "spoke in her heart; only her lips moved, but her voice was not heard." So Eli the priest thought she was drunk. However, her prayers were answered by God, and Samuel was born the next year.
(See 1 Samuel 1:1-28.)

7 Woman whose presents saved her family

David was on the warpath! He had been insulted by Nabal. David took 400 soldiers to teach Nabal a lesson. But Nabal's wife, Abigail, was smart. She quickly sent piles of food (including 200 loaves of bread) to David. The result? Nabal became ill and died. Abigail became David's wife!
(See 1 Samuel 25.)

8 Woman who painted her eyelids

Jezebel was a nasty woman. She robbed poor old Naboth of his land. She was an enemy of the godly prophet Elijah. Her last act, before she died, was to paint her eyelids and adorn her head.
(See 1 Kings 21; 2 Kings 9:30-37.)

9 Beauty queen

King Ahasuerus was very angry! His wife, Queen Vashti, would not obey him. So he sent her away. A new queen had to be named – one who was young and beautiful. Esther, a Jewish woman, was "lovely and beautiful." She became queen.
(See Esther 1:1–2:18.)

10 Unnamed maid

The commander of the Syrian army, General Naaman, was a leper. A captive Hebrew girl served Naaman's wife. The servant told Naaman to go to the Israelite prophet Elisha for healing. Naaman swallowed his pride and went. He returned healed.
(See 2 Kings 5.)

10 PROPHETS, PRIESTS, AND PREACHERS

1 Prophet who was fed by ravens

Israel was going to have a long drought. God worked out a way to keep His leading prophet alive during the drought. Elijah was told to go to live by a brook called Cherith. That gave him water. And ravens brought him bread and meat!
(See 1 Kings 17:1-7.)

2 Prophets who wanted to die

Two Old Testament men wanted to die: Elijah and Jeremiah. Jeremiah said, "Woe is me, my mother, that you have borne me."
(See 1 Kings 19:4; Jeremiah 15:10.)

3 Prophet who prophesied most about the coming of Jesus

We find about 50 quotations from the book of Isaiah in the New Testament. The New Testament writers saw how clearly Isaiah had written about Jesus Christ in his prophecy. The best place to see this is in Isaiah 52:13–53:12. There, more than 20 things listed about Jesus are all true.

4 Persecuted prophet

No wonder Jeremiah wanted to quit. He tried to preach the message God had given him. But "They took Jeremiah and cast him into the dungeon of Malchiah the king's son.... And in the dungeon there was no water, but mire. So Jeremiah sank in the mire." He was later pulled out by a man called Ebed-Melech.
(See Jeremiah 38:1-13.)

5 Actor-prophet

If your local pastor lay down on his left side for 390 days, you would wonder why. But that is what the prophet Ezekiel did. He acted out his message that Jerusalem would be attacked. Slowly, people took notice of Ezekiel.
(See Ezekiel 4:1-17.)

6 Vegetarian prophet

Daniel survived the lions' den. He became prime minister. He also wrote some amazing prophecy in his book. Part of his success lay in his diet. Daniel refused to eat the rcyal food. He said, "Give us vegetables to eat and water to drink." This was his way of showing his faith in God.
(See Daniel 1:1-21.)

7 Shepherd who became a prophet

On the night Jesus was born, Bethlehem shepherds got in on the act. Hundreds of years earlier, a shepherd lived a few miles south of Bethlehem in a place called Tekoa. He did not go to a special school for preachers or a special college for prophets. But this shepherd became Amos the prophet.
(See Amos 1:1.)

8 Prophet with an unfaithful wife

The people of Israel were being unfaithful to God. God loved them. But they turned their backs on God and broke His laws. The prophet Hosea came along. He chose an unfaithful wife, Gomer. She was always running after other men. Hosea said this was just like Israel's actions toward God and its running after false gods.
(See Hosea 1:2-4; 4:1-19.)

9 Priest who hated Jesus

Not everyone liked Jesus. The top religious leaders were often against Him. Caiaphas, the high priest, did not like Him. He "tore his clothes, saying, '[Jesus] has spoken blasphemy! . . . What do you think?'" "He is deserving of death," the other leaders answered.
(See Matthew 26:57-66.)

10 Tied-up prophet

Agabus the prophet wanted to stop Paul the preacher from going to Jerusalem and being arrested there. So "he took Paul's belt, bound his own hands and feet, and said ... 'So shall the Jews at Jerusalem bind the man who owns this belt.'" But Paul still went to Jerusalem. The prophecy came true.
(See Acts 21:10-14.)

11 HEROES AND HEROINES

1 Strongest

Samson tore a lion apart with his hands. He burst through the gates of a Philistine city. Then he killed 1,000 Philistines with the jawbone of a donkey. Finally, he pushed down the pillars of a temple. He and about 3,000 Philistines were buried alive. (See Judges 14:6; 15:15; 16:1-3, 25-30.)

2 Wisest

Solomon did not ask God to give him money, power, or a long life. Instead, he asked for an understanding mind. God granted him a wise mind, as well as money, power, and a long life. (See 1 Kings 3:11-14, 16-28; 4:29-34.)

3 Most fireproof

Nebuchadnezzar, king of Babylon, erected a golden idol. Shadrach, Meshach, and Abed-Nego refused to worship it. The angry king had them thrown into a fiery furnace. It was heated to seven times its normal temperature. However, God protected them. (See Daniel 3:1-28.)

4 Greatest warrior

Gideon – with 300 men, 300 trumpets, and God – defeated 135,000 Midianites. About 120,000 of them were killed. (See Judges 7:7-8; 8:10-12.)

5 Richest

Solomon became very, very rich. He received money from tribute, taxes, and trade. His country was so rich that silver was said to be as common as stones in Jerusalem.
(See 1 Kings 10:27.)

6 Most frequently married

King Solomon had 700 wives and 300 concubines. It is a good thing he was also the richest king!
(See 1 Kings 11:3.)

7 Most persecuted

Paul had a tough time as a follower of Christ. "Five times I received forty stripes minus one. Three times I was beaten with rods; once I was stoned … in sleeplessness often, in hunger and thirst, in fastings often, in cold and nakedness."
(See 2 Corinthians 11:24-27.)

8 Most faithful

Anna was a widow. She was an old prophetess who met the baby Jesus in the temple. For many years, she "did not depart from the temple, but served God with fastings and prayers night and day."
(See Luke 2:36-38.)

9 Martyred

Stephen was "full of faith and power." He performed "great wonders and signs among the people." One day he preached a sermon. He was stoned to death for it. Stephen is the first Christian martyr.
(See Acts 6:8–8:2.)

10 Most original killer

Sisera was Israel's enemy. Jael got him to come into her tent. She gave him a cup of milk. She settled him down for a nap. And she covered him up. Then she took a tent peg and drove it into his temple! Sisera was dead before he knew what hit him.
(See Judges 4:17-22.)

12 VILLAINS

1 Biggest

Goliath was six cubits and a span (over nine and a half feet) tall. He was the tallest Bible villain. But perhaps Og, king of Bashan, was heavier. He owned an iron bedstead that was nine cubits (over 13 feet) long and four cubits (six feet) wide.
(See 1 Samuel 17:4; Deuteronomy 3:11.)

2 Cruelest

There are many cruel villains in the Bible. One of them is Menahem, king of Israel. He attacked the city of Tiphsah and ripped open pregnant women. Another is Manasseh, king of Judah. He raised altars to false gods and burned his own sons as an offering.
(See 2 Kings 15:16; 21:6; 2 Chronicles 33:3-6.)

3 King Ahab

Evil King Ahab was bossed by his wife, the cruel Queen Jezebel. Even though he was king of Israel, Ahab built altars to the god Baal. Many Israelites turned away from worshiping God. This pleased Jezebel but displeased God.
(See 1 Kings 16:29-33.)

4 Haman

Haman hated Mordecai. So Haman used all his cunning and got the king to agree to pass a law. It said that all the Jews in his land should be killed. And, of course, Mordecai was a Jew! But Haman did not know one important fact. Mordecai had friends in high places. His cousin was married to the king.
(See Esther 5–7.)

5 Doeg the dreadful

Doeg was chief of Saul's herdsmen. Doeg told Saul that David had been helped by Ahimelech the priest. So Saul said, "You shall surely die, Ahimelech." But Saul's guards refused to kill priests. So Doeg killed Ahimelech and 85 other priests. He also killed many women, children, infants, cattle, donkeys, and sheep.
(See 1 Samuel 22:9-19.)

6 Sanballat the plotter

When Nehemiah rebuilt the walls of Jerusalem, Sanballat was angry. Sanballat tried to stop the building project. He made fun of the workers. He plotted to attack Jerusalem. And he called meetings to delay everything. Nehemiah prayed to God and got on with the work.
(See Nehemiah 4:1-23; 6:1-9.)

7 Baby-killer

King Herod's evil knew no bounds. When he found out he had been tricked by the wise men, he was very angry. He gave orders that all the boys in Bethlehem and its vicinity who were two years old and under be put to death. But Jesus, Mary, and Joseph had already escaped to Egypt.
(See Matthew 2:13-16.)

8 Jesus' betrayer

The Jewish leaders agreed: Judas would betray Jesus. They even worked out the secret signal – a kiss. So the chief priests gave Judas 30 silver coins. Later, Judas went right to Jesus and kissed him. And Jesus was arrested.
(See Matthew 26:14-16, 47-56.)

9 Dying thief

The two men crucified with Jesus were criminals. But one of them said to Jesus, "Lord, remember me." Jesus said, "Today you will be with Me in Paradise."
(See Luke 23:42-43.)

10 Elymas the sorcerer

The setting was the island of Paphos. The governor wanted to hear the word of God. Barnabas and Paul were about to preach. Elymas the sorceror stepped in. He tried to turn the governor away from the Christian faith. Immediately Elymas became blind.
(See Acts 13:6-12.)

13 BATTLES AND WARRIORS

1 Fall of Jericho

For six days Joshua and the Israelite army marched around Jericho. The soldiers marched quietly while seven priests blew seven trumpets. Then on the seventh day, the priests blew the trumpets again. The soldiers shouted. And the walls of the city fell down.
(See Joshua 6:1-20.)

2 Military man's motto

We find the motto of Joshua in God's words to him. God said, "Be strong and of good courage; do not be afraid, nor be dismayed, for the LORD your God is with you wherever you go."
(See Joshua 1:9.)

3 Trumpets and torches

Gideon's 300 men defeated the huge Midianite army. Gideon's army held torches in their left hands and trumpets in their right hands. Then they shouted, "The sword of the LORD and of Gideon!" The Midianites fled in fear.
(See Judges 7:1-22.)

4 Samson the strong

Samson had his own way of dealing with the Philistines. The men of Judah tied Samson up with two new ropes. Then they turned him over to the Philistines. Samson snapped the ropes. Then, with a donkey's jawbone, he killed 1,000 Philistines.
(See Judges 15.)

5 Secret of Samson's strength

Samson attacked the Philistines by himself. He seemed like the strongest man in the world. But the secret of his strength was not in his muscles. It was in his trust in God. On the last day of his life, he prayed, "O Lord GOD, remember me, I pray! Strengthen me, I pray, just this once, O God."
(See Judges 16:28.)

6 David the warrior

David was a mighty warrior. Second Samuel 8:5 says, "When the Syrians of Damascus came to help Hadadezer king of Zobah, David killed twenty-two thousand of the Syrians."

7 Fall of Samaria

Samaria was the capital of the northern kingdom, Israel. It fell to Sargon, king of Assyria, in 721 B.C. That was the end of 10 of the tribes of Israel.

8 Fall of Jerusalem

The Babylonian king Nebuchadnezzar attacked and destroyed Jerusalem in 587 B.C. He sent many Jews to exile in Babylon. This was a sad time in the history of the Jews. It happened because of their unfaithfulness to God.
(See Jeremiah 52.)

9 Be like a soldier

Wear a soldier's armor, said the apostle Paul. He saw the Christian life as a spiritual battle. He said to be ready for the fight. "Put on the whole armor of God … having girded your waist with truth, having put on the breastplate of righteousness … the shield of faith … the helmet of salvation."
(See Ephesians 6:10-20.)

14 COMMANDS

1 Ten Commandments
The Ten Commandments show the way for individuals and groups to live. The first four commands tell how to live with God. The last six are about parents, murder, adultery, stealing, giving false testimony, and coveting. They tell how to live with others.
(See Exodus 20.)

2 Jesus' two greatest commandments
Jesus summed up the Ten Commandments, the Law, and the Prophets in this way: "Love the LORD your God with all your heart, with all your soul, and with all your mind. . . . Love your neighbor as yourself."
(See Matthew 22:37-40.)

3 Jesus' new commandment
Jesus gave one new commandment to his disciples, "Love one another; as I have loved you … you also love one another."
(See John 13:34.)

4 Commandments about the devil
The Bible does not tell what the devil looks like. But it does take the devil seriously. James and Peter explain how you can get the better of the devil. "Resist the devil and he will flee from you." "Be sober, be vigilant; because your adversary the devil walks about like a roaring lion, seeking whom he may devour. Resist him, steadfast in the faith."
(See James 4:7; 1 Peter 5:8-9.)

5 Commandment to forgive
Jesus made it clear that we must forgive. He said, "Forgive, and you will be forgiven." So forgiving others is the first step in seeking God's forgiveness. But knowing that does not make forgiving easy.
(See Luke 6:37.)

6 Commandment about people in need

James had a good idea about people in need. "If a brother or sister is naked and destitute of daily food, and one of you says to them, 'Depart in peace, be warmed and filled,' but you do not give them the things which are needed for the body, what does it profit?"
(See James 2:15-16.)

7 Commandment about humility

There's a good reason to seek humility, Peter said. "Humble yourselves under the mighty hand of God, that He may exalt you in due time."
(See 1 Peter 5:6.)

10 Commandment to endure

The writer of Hebrews and Jesus teach that the Christian life is a race. It is not a sprint but a marathon. "You have need of endurance." "He who endures to the end shall be saved."
(See Hebrews 10:36; Matthew 24:13.)

8 Commandment about rulers

Human rulers are often selfish and unjust. Still, Paul insists, "Let every soul be subject to the governing authorities. For there is no authority except from God."
(See Romans 13:1.)

9 What to do with heretics

Heretics are not to be ignored. The apostle of love says: "Many deceivers have gone out into the world who do not confess Jesus Christ as coming in the flesh. . . . Do not receive [such a person] into your house nor greet him."
(See 2 John 7, 10.)

15 GOD AT WORK

1 Creation

"In the beginning God…" is the first statement of the Bible. Everything that has been created – geological, geographical, animal, and human – is made by God's power.
(See Genesis 1:1-31.)

2 Bringing good out of evil

Joseph was sold into slavery by his jealous brothers. You would not think that any good could come from it. But Joseph said, "You meant evil against me; but God meant it for good, in order to … save many people."
(See Genesis 50:20.)

3 Using a pagan king

King Cyrus of Persia was not an Israelite. He didn't worship God. But God used Cyrus. Cyrus allowed the Israelites to return from exile. He even helped them. He said, "Go up to Jerusalem … and build the house of the LORD."
(See Ezra 1:3.)

4 Against all odds

The writer of Lamentations was upset. God's special city of Jerusalem was in ruins. The few Israelites who hadn't been exiled had no food to eat. The future looked hopeless. And yet one of the most hopeful verses in the Bible comes in the middle of all this: "Through the LORD's mercies we are not consumed, because His compassions fail not."
(See Lamentations 3:22.)

5 Text of one-syllable words

The deepest statement of all time was expressed by Jesus in a sentence of one-syllable words. "The Son of Man has come to seek and to save that which was lost."
(See Luke 19:10.)

7 Saddest day

The day of Jesus' crucifixion was the saddest day ever. And yet it was not. The killing of an innocent person is bad. But the death of the perfect, sinless Son of God in the place of sinners turns out to be good. (See 1 Peter 2:24.)

8 Christ's resurrection

Jesus Christ was dead and in a tomb. That was the end of the story for most people. Still, a tough Roman guard was placed at the door of the tomb – just in case the disciples tried to steal the body. In this hopeless situation, God acted. He raised Jesus to life again. (See 1 Corinthians 15:20-28.)

6 Teenager against giant

No one thought little David had a chance against nine-foot-tall Goliath. But one smooth stone and a sling became a lethal weapon. David tells how he won the fight: "All this assembly shall know that the LORD does not save with sword and spear; for the battle is the LORD's." (See 1 Samuel 17:47.)

9 Spiritual birth

Churchgoers used to get fed up with preacher John Wesley. He preached from the same Bible text again and again. He said, "I will not preach on 'ye must be born again' once I know you have been born again." He knew that Jesus said this can only happen when people are "born of the Spirit." (See John 3:5-8.)

16 STRANGE EVENTS

MENE MENE TEKEL UPHARSIN

1 Handwriting on the wall

"The handwriting is on the wall" is a well-known saying. It comes from a story in Daniel. The fingers of a human hand appeared and wrote on a wall. During King Belshazzar's banquet, they wrote the puzzling statement "MENE, MENE, TEKEL, UPHARSIN." This was meant to humble this godless king. (See Daniel 5:1-31.)

2 Night the lions didn't eat

The lions were not full or on a hunger strike the night Daniel was thrown into their den. God's angel "shut the lions' mouths." The result? Pagan King Darius proclaimed that his people "must tremble and fear before the God of Daniel." (See Daniel 6:1-28.)

3 Day the sun stood still

Joshua 10:12-14 tells of this strange event. As Israel defeated the Amorites, "The sun stood still, and the moon stopped, till the people had revenge upon their enemies."

4 Day the sun went backward

Now this really does give scientists a headache. God gave a sign that King Hezekiah would be healed and given extra time to live. The sun's shadow moved backward ten steps on the stairway of Ahaz. (See 2 Kings 20:1-11.)

5 Woman who became a pillar of salt

The cities of Sodom and Gomorrah were full of evil, sexual sin, and godlessness. Lot's wife could not resist looking back when God destroyed the two cities because of their evil. Genesis 19:26 does not tell how, but Lot's wife "became a pillar of salt" for looking back.

6 Lazarus lives again

Mary, Martha, and their brother Lazarus were close friends of Jesus. Lazarus died. Four days later Jesus arrived. He did what seemed impossible. Jesus said to the dead body in the tomb, "Lazarus, come forth!" And out came Lazarus, looking like a walking bandage. (See John 11:1-44.)

7 Eutychus

This young man is famous because he fell asleep during a sermon by Paul. He was sitting in a window. He fell to his death from the third floor. Then Paul went down to him, hugged him, and brought him back to life. (See Acts 20:7-12.)

8 Blinded army

Elisha was in the town of Dothan. Syrian soldiers were all around it. The king of Syria wanted to capture him. But Elisha had a secret weapon. Second Kings 6:18 tells what happened: "When the Syrians came down to him, Elisha prayed to the LORD, and said, 'Strike this people … with blindness.' And He struck them with blindness."

9 Fish story?

This story would be hard to believe if it were not told by Jesus Christ. He said to Peter, "Go to the sea, cast in a hook, and take the fish that comes up first. And when you have opened its mouth, you will find a piece of money; take that and give it to them for Me and you." (See Matthew 17:27.)

17 NUMBERS

1 Book of Numbers
One book in the Bible is called Numbers. It gets its name from the fact that it contains so many numbers. It tells the number of Israelites who were counted in a census: 601,730 to be exact. (See Numbers 26:1-51.)

2 Special numbers: 1
The Bible uses the number 1 to teach that God is one, and He is the only God. Jesus and God the Father are one. Christians are all one body. The number 1 also teaches that sin came into the world through one person. The human race can also be traced back to one person. (See Deuteronomy 6:4; John 10:30; 17:21; Romans 5:12; Acts 17:26.)

3 Special numbers: 7
The number 7 appears many times in the Bible. It is often linked to the ideas of perfection and completion. General Naaman had to dip himself in the Jordan seven times. The priests and soldiers marched around Jericho seven times. The psalmist even praised God seven times a day. (See 2 Kings 5:10; Joshua 6:4; Psalm 119:164.)

4 Special numbers: 12
There were 12 tribes of Israel. There were 12 disciples. This sheds light on one of the most puzzling questions of all time. Why does God seem to choose some people and not others? The choice of the 12 tribes and 12 disciples underlines one fact: they were all chosen because of God's kindness, not because they were special in themselves. (See Genesis 49:28; Matthew 10:1.)

5 Special numbers: 40
The Bible often uses the number 40. It often means God is about to usher in some new event or era. So the rain during the Flood lasted 40 days. The spies explored Canaan for 40 days. Jonah warned Nineveh for 40 days. And Jesus fasted in the wilderness for 40 days. (See Genesis 7:17; Numbers 13:25; Jonah 3:4; Matthew 4:2.)

6 Two quarreling Christians

Imagine being remembered for arguing. That's how we recall the two quarreling Christians in Philippians 4:2. Paul said, "I implore Euodia and I implore Syntyche to be of the same mind in the Lord."

7 Eight survivors of the flood

We usually say that nearly every living thing was killed by the Flood. But we could say that God rescued eight people from the Flood: Noah and his wife; their three sons, Shem, Ham, and Japheth; and their sons' wives. That was probably how the eight felt – like survivors.
(See Genesis 6–8.)

8 666

The number given to the beast in Revelation 13:18 is 666. Writers have used oceans of ink trying to identify him. The author of Revelation says this beast is powerful, deceitful, and able to perform miracles. But he does not reveal his identity.
(See Revelation 13:11-18.)

18 INTERESTING FACTS

1 First rainbow

The Bible tells about the first rainbow. Now, all rainbows are special. God said, "I set My rainbow in the cloud, and it shall be for the sign of the covenant between Me and the earth." This was just after the Flood. So it is easy to see why Noah knew the rainbow was a sign of God's love for him and his family.
(See Genesis 9:8-17.)

2 "Do not be afraid"

This command appears in the Bible 365 times. That's one way God tells us to trust Him each day of the year.
(See Luke 1:30 [and the other 364 references].)

3 First and last

The first book of the Bible tells of a serpent's tempting Eve. The last book of the Bible calls Satan "that serpent of old, who is the Devil."
(See Genesis 3; Revelation 20:2.)

5 Seven hundred left-handed stone-slingers

Perhaps Goliath would not have been so brave in his fight with David if he had known this verse:
"Among all this people were seven hundred select men who were left-handed; every one could sling a stone at a hair's breadth and not miss."
(See Judges 20:16.)

4 Water and fire

The Flood in Noah's day is a picture of God's judgment on the earth. The day of God's last judgment will be brought about by fire. "The elements will melt with fervent heat; both the earth and the works that are in it will be burned up."
(See 2 Peter 3:10.)

6 Jonah and the whale?

It sounds like a very fishy tale. But the Bible word used in Jonah's story does not mean "whale." It means "a very large fish." The type of fish is not important. The point is that this fish was part of God's plan to save runaway Jonah.
(See the book of Jonah.)

7 Only named ship in the Bible

There is only one ship called by name in the Bible. It is the one Paul took on his voyage to Rome. It was "an Alexandrian ship whose figurehead was the Twin Brothers."
(See Acts 28:11.)

8 Urim and Thummim

The Urim and Thummim were carried by Aaron in his high priest's breastplate. No one knows what they were exactly or how they worked. All we know is that they were used to learn God's will. "He shall stand before Eleazar the priest, who shall inquire before the LORD for him by the judgment of the Urim."
(See Numbers 27:21.)

9 Tree of Genesis and Revelation

In Genesis God told Adam and Eve not to eat the fruit of the tree in the midst of the garden. The trees in Revelation are described in this way: "On either side of the river, was the tree of life, which bore twelve fruits, each tree yielding its fruit every month. The leaves of the tree were for the healing of the nations."
(See Genesis 3:1-7; Revelation 22:2.)

19 JOURNEYS

1 Dry ground through the sea
By a miracle, the Israelites escaped the Egyptian horsemen and chariots. "The children of Israel went into the midst of the sea on the dry ground, and the waters were a wall to them on their right hand and on their left." (See Exodus 14.)

2 On the run from a wicked queen
Queen Jezebel caused Elijah to fear for his life. She once threatened to kill him. Elijah ran for his life. He ended up in a desert, under a broom tree. There, he felt like dying. But an angel helped him. Elijah was given a cake of bread baked on coals, a jar of water, and some sleep. (See 1 Kings 19:1-9.)

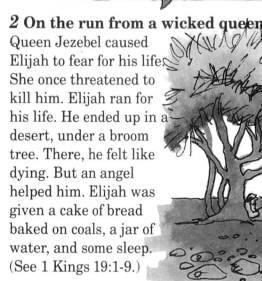

3 Mary's famous donkey ride
The Bible never says that Mary rode a donkey. But how else could a woman who was about to have a baby travel from Nazareth to Bethlehem? Of course, if Joseph and Mary had been rich, they would have traveled by horse and chariot. (See Luke 2:1-7.)

4 Most humble donkey ride
For hundreds of years the Jews had been waiting for their savior. They thought he would rid them of the Romans and take Jerusalem by storm. Most of them did not know the Savior of the world as He rode in on Palm Sunday. He was on the animal poor people used – a donkey. (See Luke 19:28-44.)

5 Chariot ride that ended in a conversion
The Ethiopian official must have been very rich. Only rich people rode in traveling chariots. "The Spirit said to Philip, 'Go near and overtake this chariot.'" The man just "happened" to be reading from Isaiah. Before long, Philip "preached Jesus to him" and baptized him. (See Acts 8:26-40.)

6 Paul's travels

No one in the New Testament went through more dangers in travel than the apostle Paul. Eight times in 2 Corinthians 11:25-26 he says he was "in perils." "Three times I was shipwrecked; a night and a day I have been in the deep; in journeys often, in perils of waters, in perils of robbers, in perils of my own countrymen, in perils of the Gentiles, in perils in the city, in perils in the wilderness, in perils in the sea, in perils among false brethren."

7 Wilderness journey

Because they disobeyed God, the people of Israel had to wander in the desert for 40 years. They could not enter the promised land right away. During this time, God gave them quail and manna to eat. Twice, water came from a rock for them to drink. In the Bible, the desert and wilderness are places where people are taught by God.

8 Night escape for the baby Jesus

Herod the king was about to kill all boys two years and under who lived in Bethlehem. An angel warned Joseph in a dream. So Joseph took Mary and Jesus by night to Egypt to escape this mass killing.
(See Matthew 2:13-18.)

9 On the way to Jerusalem

Jesus was on His way to Jerusalem and His crucifixion. He passed through Jericho. A blind man there asked Jesus to heal him. Jesus healed him. Bartimaeus, the man who could now see, followed Jesus to Jerusalem. It was a trip that he would never forget.
(See Mark 10:46-52.)

10 Roads of Jesus' day

There were no roads, as we know them today, in Bible times. The 50,000-mile network of Roman roads reached Palestine only after Jesus' death. Until then most "roads" were little more than paths. The biggest boulders were removed. The deepest potholes were filled. Unless you had to, you just did not travel.

20 BUILDINGS

1 Tower to reach the sky

The town with the biggest tower was famous in the times of Genesis. Genesis 11:3 states the aim of the tower of Babel: "Come, let us build ourselves a city, and a tower whose top is in the heavens; let us make a name for ourselves." God was not pleased.
(See Genesis 11:1-9.)

2 Solomon's temple

Solomon spared no expense to build the temple. He brought cedar and cypress wood and special stone from Lebanon. The whole building and its courts and furniture were beautiful. But best of all, God filled it with His presence on the day it was dedicated.
(See 1 Kings 6–9.)

3 Solomon's palace

The truth is that Solomon took more care on his own buildings than on God's temple. His own throne was made with ivory, overlaid with fine gold. The throne had six steps. Its back had a rounded top. On both sides of the seat were armrests. A lion stood beside each of them.
(See 1 Kings 10.)

4 Herod's temple

King Herod built a temple to his own glory. The building itself was one of the largest in the ancient world. For Jesus' judgment of it, read Matthew 24:2. He knew that the Romans would destroy the temple. So Jesus said that one stone would not be left upon another.

5 House with a hole in the roof

It was not a leaking roof. In fact, it did not have a hole in it until the day Jesus visited. Four faithful friends were eager to bring their sick friend to Jesus. But they were blocked from the front door of the house by all the people. So they went up on the flat roof. They made a hole in it. Then they let their friend down to the feet of Jesus.
(See Mark 2:1-12.)

6 Building that was pushed down single-handedly

Yes, this is the story of Samson's death. His eyes had been put out. But the boy who led him around helped him find two pillars of the pagan temple. Samson pushed the pillars down. He and about 3,000 Philistines were buried alive. (See Judges 16:23-31.)

8 Building where Jesus was born

This takes a little bit of thought. The only clue we have about the building where Jesus was born is in Luke 2:7. Mary "wrapped Him in swaddling cloths, and laid Him in a manger, because there was no room for them in the inn." The most likely place to find a manger is a stable.

7 Prison that had an earthquake

Now here is a strange way to break out of prison. Paul and Silas were singing hymns in prison. Then a violent earthquake shook the prison to its foundation. The prison doors opened. The jailer nearly took his own life when he saw this. But he ended up being baptized instead.
(See Acts 16:22-40.)

9 City with no temple

Heaven will be a square city of "pure gold, like clear glass." But there will be no temple. In his vision, John says, "I saw no temple in it, for the Lord God Almighty and the Lamb are its temple."
(See Revelation 21:1-27.)

21 WEATHER

1 World's biggest flood

This was *some* rain. For 40 days the Flood kept coming. It covered the mountains to a depth of more than 20 feet. And it killed everything that moved. The floodwaters lasted for 150 days. Noah had been faithful to God. When told to do what seemed crazy, he built an ark. Now he knew that God knew best.
(See Genesis 6–9.)

2 Parting of a sea

The Exodus was quite surprising. "The waters were divided. So the children of Israel went into the midst of the sea on the dry ground, and the waters were a wall to them on their right hand and on their left." A little later, the waters rushed back. They drowned the Egyptian army.
(See Exodus 14.)

4 Storms on the Sea of Galilee

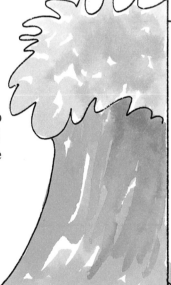

People on the Sea of Galilee often saw sudden storms. Jesus was sleeping in a boat during such a storm. The disciples thought they were going to drown. The boat was filling with water, and the wind was blowing. They woke Jesus up. He rebuked the wind and water, and all was calm.
(See Luke 8:22-25.)

3 Drought

Elijah said to Ahab, "As the LORD God of Israel lives, before whom I stand, there shall not be dew nor rain these years, except at my word." The drought was a sign to the wicked King Ahab. The drought took place, but Ahab had a hard heart.
(See 1 Kings 17.)

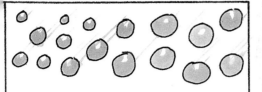

5 Worst hailstorm ever?

The seventh of the ten plagues was perhaps the worst hailstorm ever. "And the hail struck throughout the whole land of Egypt, all that was in the field, both man and beast; and the hail struck every herb of the field and broke every tree of the field." (See Exodus 9:13-35.)

6 Weather as Jesus was crucified

The darkest day in history was when the Son of God was crucified. Luke tells about the moment. "It was about the sixth hour, and there was darkness over all the earth until the ninth hour." (See Luke 23:44-45.)

7 Proverbs about the weather

"When it is evening you say, 'It will be fair weather, for the sky is red'; and in the morning, 'It will be foul weather today, for the sky is red and threatening.' Hypocrites! You know how to discern the face of the sky, but you cannot discern the signs of the times." This is what Jesus told the Pharisees and Sadducees. (See Matthew 16:1-3.)

8 Sea calmed by throwing a man overboard

God told Jonah to go inland to the city of Nineveh. Jonah went down to the port of Joppa. He got on a boat to take him to the other side of the world, to Tarshish. The terrible storm at sea stopped the moment the crew threw Jonah into the water. The rest of the story everyone knows. (See Jonah 1–4.)

22 PLACES

1 City on a hill
Jerusalem was the city of peace. It sat on Palestine's high mountain ridge. That is some 2,500 feet above sea level. It was not good for farming and did not have enough water. But it lay in the path of a major trade route.

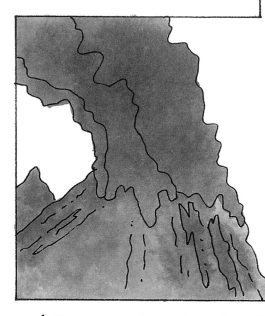

2 Mountain of the Ten Commandments
Certain mountains were important in the history of the Israelites. Moses went up Mount Sinai and twice received the Ten Commandments. The Israelites understood that something important was happening. As Exodus 20:18 records, "All the people witnessed the thunderings, the lightning flashes, the sound of the trumpet, and the mountain smoking; and when the people saw it, they trembled and stood afar off."

3 Mountain of Jesus' transfiguration
We don't know the name of the place of Jesus' transfiguration. We know only that He took Peter, James, and John and "led them up on a high mountain by themselves." Some people think the transfiguration took place on Mount Tabor. Jesus' face shone like the sun, and His clothes became white as light.
(See Matthew 17:1-2.)

4 Mountain where Jesus loved to pray
When Jesus was near Jerusalem, He liked to pray on the Mount of Olives. Jesus was arrested there. He often prayed in Gethsemane, which means "olive press." There, Judas betrayed him with a kiss. Clearly Judas knew where he would find Jesus.
(See Matthew 26:36-56.)

5 City full of idols

What brings tears to your eyes? Well, the sight of Athens made the apostle Paul sad. He could not bear the city being full of idols. He even found an altar inscribed: "TO THE UNKNOWN GOD." Paul set about putting things right. He preached in the synagogue and marketplace and at the meeting of the Areopagus.
(See Acts 17:16-34.)

6 Riot against the gospel

When personal interests are threatened, the Christian message comes under fire. The problem in Ephesus centered around "a certain man named Demetrius, a silversmith, who made silver shrines of Diana." This brought in "no small profit to the craftsmen." Paul said that handmade gods are not gods at all. The place broke out in a riot.
(See Acts 19:23-41.)

8 Two most wicked cities?

Sodom and Gomorrah were known for evil. Even two angels who came to Sodom were not safe from the evil intentions of "the men of Sodom, both old and young." No wonder God destroyed these cities.
(See Genesis 19:1-29.)

7 Center of the world

All roads led to Rome. That is not surprising really. The Romans were the first to build roads. They made over 50,000 miles of them. Paul had his heart set on preaching in Rome. The last verses of Acts might seem to be sad. Paul is confined in house arrest for two years. But in reality this was the high point in Paul's life.
(See Acts 28:23-31.)

9 Hill of Jesus' crucifixion

"There is a green hill far away, without a city wall..." goes the well-known hymn. *Without* is old-fashioned English for "outside." It was outside the walls of Jerusalem on a hill called Golgotha – "place of a skull" – that Jesus was crucified. It was some way from the center of Jerusalem. Simon from Cyrene was forced to help carry Jesus' cross.
(See Matthew 27:32-35; Mark 15:21-24.)

23 DREAMS

1 Old Testament dreamer

Joseph just could not keep his dreams to himself. "Please hear this dream which I have dreamed: There we were, binding sheaves in the field. Then behold, my sheaf arose and also stood upright; and indeed your sheaves stood all around and bowed down to my sheaf." This sums up the story of Joseph's life.
(See Genesis 37.)

2 Dream of Gideon's enemies

Gideon heard two of his enemies talking. One was telling the other about his dream. "He said, 'I have had a dream: To my surprise, a loaf of barley bread tumbled into the camp of Midian; it came to a tent and struck it so that it fell and overturned, and the tent collapsed.'" The other man knew that this meant Gideon's army would defeat the Midianites. Gideon worshiped God and won one of the biggest battles in history.
(See Judges 7.)

3 Dream that ended with long fingernails

King Nebuchadnezzar had a dream. Daniel told him its meaning. It came true immediately. Nebuchadnezzar "was driven from men and ate grass like oxen; his body was wet with the dew of heaven till his hair had grown like eagles' feathers and his nails like birds' claws."
(See Daniel 4.)

4 Dream that helped two people in love

It is a serious matter to be pregnant before you are married. Mary and Joseph were engaged. Joseph knew that Mary was pregnant but not through him. Then an angel came to Joseph in a dream. "Joseph, ... do not be afraid to take to you Mary your wife, for that which is conceived in her is of the Holy Spirit." Then follows one of the best-known Christmas verses. "She will bring forth a Son, and you shall call His name Jesus, for He will save His people from their sins."
(See Matthew 1:18-21.)

5 Dream that saved baby Jesus

Many people around the baby Jesus seem to have had dreams. The baby Jesus was in danger from the evil King Herod. He escaped to Egypt with Mary and Joseph. An angel of the Lord had come to Joseph in a dream. "Arise, take the young Child and His mother, flee to Egypt, and stay there until I bring you word; for Herod will seek the young Child to destroy Him." (See Matthew 2:13.)

6 Pilate's wife's dream

We only know one thing about Pilate's wife – she had a dream. Jesus was before Pilate, who sat on the judge's seat. Pilate's wife sent him this message: "Have nothing to do with that just Man, for I have suffered many things today in a dream because of Him." Pilate ignored his wife and listened to the Jewish leaders. (See Matthew 27:19.)

7 Dream that made a prisoner prime minister

Joseph was in an Egyptian prison. Pharaoh had a dream. He did not know what it meant. His chief butler remembered Joseph. When the butler was in prison, Joseph had told him the meaning of his dream. So Joseph was rushed from prison to the palace. He was able to tell the meaning of Pharaoh's dream (with God's help). So Joseph was put in charge of all Egypt. (See Genesis 41.)

8 Peter's trance

It was not really a dream. Peter went up on the roof to pray. He was very hungry. He fell into a trance and had a vision. The vision made Peter see that Christianity was for everyone, not just for Jews. The first person to benefit from this vision was the soldier Cornelius. Peter visited him. He told him the good news of "peace through Jesus Christ." Then he baptized this non-Jew. A few days before, Peter would not even have entered Cornelius's house. (See Acts 10.)

24 NEW TESTAMENT MEN

1 Twelve disciples

When Jesus began His public ministry, He chose 12 disciples: Simon, whom He named Peter; James the son of Zebedee and his brother John; Andrew; Philip; Bartholomew; Matthew; Thomas; James the son of Alphaeus; Thaddaeus; Simon the Cananite; and Judas Iscariot, who betrayed Jesus. As was usual in those days, these disciples lived with their teacher. They were with Him all the time.
(See Mark 3:16-19.)

2 Inner three

Three disciples – Peter, James, and John – formed the close inner circle. They were the three who saw Jesus' transfiguration. And they were the three Jesus took with Him as He prayed in Gethsemane.
(See Matthew 17:1-13; 26:36-46.)

3 Only man who went away from Jesus sad

Some people left Jesus in anger. The Pharisees and Sadducees did. But only one person went away from Jesus sad. A rich young man came to Jesus and asked, "Teacher, what good thing shall I do that I may have eternal life?" "Sell what you have and give to the poor," Jesus told him. "When the young man heard that saying, he went away sorrowful, for he had great possessions."
(See Matthew 19:16-22.)

4 Disciple who betrayed Jesus

Being one of the 12 disciples made no difference to Judas. He still betrayed Jesus. The saddest thing about Judas's story is that he didn't repent of his betrayal. Instead he went and hanged himself. He was filled with remorse.
(See Matthew 27:1-10.)

5 First missionary

Paul had hard times as a pioneer missionary. "I have been … in perils of waters, in perils of robbers, in perils of my own countrymen, in perils of the Gentiles, in perils in the city, in perils in the wilderness, in perils in the sea, in perils among false brethren; in weariness and toil, in sleeplessness often, in hunger and thirst, in fastings often." (See 2 Corinthians 11:23-27.)

6 Beheaded preacher

John the Baptist would not keep quiet when he saw evil. He called the religious leaders a "brood of vipers." Then Herod Antipas put John in prison. John had said that Herod's marriage to Herodias, his brother's wife, was wrong. John had a blunt way of talking. "It is not lawful for you to have your brother's wife," he boomed. Still, Herod was "exceedingly sorry" when Herodias's daughter asked for John's head – to be served on a platter. (See Mark 6:14-29.)

7 Man who visited Jesus at night

Nicodemus could have seen Jesus in the daytime quite easily. But John tells us that he came to Jesus "by night." Nicodemus was a leading teacher in Israel. Perhaps he did not want to be seen with this despised preacher. Nicodemus did not become Jesus' follower right away. But we do know that Nicodemus stood up for Jesus in front of other religious leaders. He also helped Joseph of Arimathea bury Jesus' body. (See John 3:1-21; 7:45-52; 19:38-42.)

8 Doctor who wrote more of the New Testament than anyone else

Who wrote more of the New Testament than anyone else? Most people would say Paul – because of all his letters. Or John – because of his three letters, his gospel, and the book of Revelation. But Luke wrote not only a gospel but also Acts. In Luke 1:3, Luke tells us that he had "perfect understanding of all things from the very first." Luke wrote true history. He has been proved right time and again.

25 NEW TESTAMENT WOMEN

1 Aged prophetess

Anna is in the New Testament once. She met the baby Jesus when He was being presented in the temple. "She was of a great age." She lived with her husband for seven years before becoming a widow. She was eighty-four when she met Jesus.
(See Luke 2:36-38.)

2 Jesus' mother

The Bible tells us little about Mary. But Luke shows us Mary's faith and character. Her response to the amazing words of the angel (that she was to be the mother of "the Son of the Highest") tells a lot. "Mary said, 'Behold the maidservant of the Lord! Let it be to me according to your word.' And the angel departed from her." Mary's song comes later. It shows more of her faith in God.
(See Luke 1:29-56.)

3 Woman who was too busy

Jesus was good friends with the sisters Mary and Martha. He often visited their home in Bethany. Bethany was a "suburb" of Jerusalem. Jesus also loved their brother Lazarus. Once Jesus gently rebuked Martha. Martha was busy with all the preparations that had to be made. She even said to Jesus, "Lord, do You not care that my sister has left me to serve alone? Therefore tell her to help me." Mary was sitting at Jesus' feet, listening to Him. Jesus replied, "You are worried and troubled about many things. But one thing is needed, and Mary has chosen that good part."
(See Luke 10:38-42.)

4 Grandmother

Timothy, thanks to Paul's help, became a missionary and preacher. Paul once wrote to him about his faith in God. He said that this faith had also been with his mother, Eunice, and his grandmother Lois. That is three generations of believers.
(See 2 Timothy 1:3-7.)

5 Peter's mother-in-law

Some people believed that each of the 12 disciples was unmarried. But Peter was not. The Bible mentions his mother-in-law. She shows up with a high fever in Luke 4:38-39. Jesus bends over her and rebukes the fever. Then the fever leaves her.

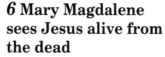

6 Mary Magdalene sees Jesus alive from the dead

Mary was very, very sad. She stood outside Jesus' tomb and wept. She was asked, "Why are you weeping?" She thought the man who asked was the gardener. But then the man called her by name. And she knew He was Jesus.
(See John 20:11-18.)

7 Woman who liked sewing

Her name was Tabitha, or Dorcas (which means *gazelle*). She was known in Joppa for doing good and helping the poor. She made robes and other clothing for the needy. She died, but Peter brought her back to life. As a result, "many believed on the Lord."
(See Acts 9:26-43.)

8 Generous widow

This unknown widow has become famous. From her, we get our phrase "the widow's mite." She would have been amazed that anyone saw her put two small copper coins in the temple treasury. But Jesus saw it. He saw beyond the money to the poor widow's heart. He said, "This poor widow has put in more than all; for all these out of their abundance have put in offerings for God, but she out of her poverty put in all the livelihood that she had."
(See Luke 21:1-4.)

26 ANIMALS, BIRDS, AND REPTILES

1 Ram that saved Isaac's life

Abraham had made up his mind. The Lord had told him to offer his son Isaac as a burnt offering. Abraham built the altar. He arranged the wood on it. He tied Isaac up. He put Isaac on the wood. Then he held the knife in his hand ready to kill him. What drama! And then the angel of the Lord called, "Abraham, Abraham!...Do not lay your hand on the lad ... now I know that you fear God, since you have not withheld your son, your only son, from Me." Then Abraham saw a ram caught by its horns in a bush. So he sacrificed the ram instead of Isaac.
(See Genesis 22.)

2 First bird out of the ark

The ark had come to rest on the mountains of Ararat. The waters were going down, so Noah sent out a raven from the ark. But it was too early. The raven kept on flying around because there was still water everywhere.
(See Genesis 8:1-7.)

3 Second bird out of the ark

Along with the raven, Noah also sent out a dove. But it couldn't find anywhere to rest either. So Noah brought it back into the ark. Seven days later, Noah sent the dove out again. This time the dove came back with a fresh olive leaf in its beak. After another week, Noah let the dove out once more. This time it did not return. Life in the ark was over.
(See Genesis 8:6-22.)

4 Birds that became food for the wandering Israelites

The Israelites longed for meat to eat in the wilderness. "Who will give us meat to eat? We remember the fish which we ate freely in Egypt, the cucumbers, the melons, the leeks, the onions, and the garlic." They seemed to forget about making bricks without straw and being treated as slaves. Anyway, God did answer their grumbling. He gave them a tasty game bird – quail.
(See Numbers 11:4-35.)

5 Snake that bit Paul

Paul often rolled up his sleeves to get jobs done. Once he was collecting some firewood while on the island of Malta. A poisonous snake bit Paul's hand. The islanders expected Paul to drop dead. They thought that he was a murderer who was being punished. Paul shook the snake off into the fire. He did not suffer any harm. Then the people thought that he was a god. (See Acts 28:1-6.)

6 Bronze snake

The Israelites were being bitten by deadly serpents in the wilderness. The Lord told Moses to make a fiery serpent and to place it on the top of a pole in the camp. People who looked at the bronze serpent lived even though they had been bitten. Jesus once compared this to His being lifted up on the cross. People look to Him and have their sins forgiven. (See Numbers 21:4-9; John 3:14-15.)

7 Learning from the ant

The book of Proverbs has many wise sayings. One is, "Go to the ant, you sluggard! Consider her ways and be wise, which, having no captain, overseer or ruler, provides her supplies in the summer, and gathers her food in the harvest." (See Proverbs 6:6-8.)

8 "Look at the birds of the air"

Jesus once gave this advice. Think about how God gives the birds their food. Will your heavenly Father not look after you? Does He not love you more than He loves the birds? That was the point of Jesus' words. Jesus was teaching people not to worry but to place their trust in God. (See Matthew 6:25-27.)

27 BIBLE CHILDREN AND YOUNG PEOPLE

1 Boy who heard God speaking to him

The first time Samuel heard God calling him, he ran to the elderly Eli. He said, "Here I am, for you called me." Eli replied, "I did not call; lie down again." This happened twice more. Then Eli told Samuel to say, "Speak, LORD, for Your servant hears." Samuel did this, and he received God's message for Eli.
(See 1 Samuel 3.)

2 Boy who hid

Saul was about to be chosen as king. But no one could find him. Now Saul was not the sort of person you could miss in a crowd. He was head and shoulders taller than anyone else. Eventually they found him hiding among the equipment.
(See 1 Samuel 10:17-27.)

3 Boy whose lunch Jesus used

The crowd was hungry. Jesus asked His disciples, as a test, "Where shall we buy bread, that these may eat?" Philip was sure it was beyond their means. He replied, "Two hundred denarii worth of bread is not sufficient for them, that every one of them may have a little." Andrew had found a boy who had five barley loaves and two small fish. But how far would they go among so many? Jesus used them for a miracle. He fed 5,000 people. And all the crowd had plenty to eat.
(See John 6:1-14.)

4 Boy who saved Paul's life

He must have had sharp ears and a brave heart. Paul's nephew overheard a plot to kill Paul. He went to the barracks where Paul was a prisoner and told him. Paul sent his nephew with a centurion to the commander of the soldiers. Clearly this commander knew how to treat people. He was a powerful man. But he "took him by the hand, went aside, and asked privately, 'What is it that you have to tell me?'" The plot against Paul's life was foiled.
(See Acts 23:12-24.)

5 Girl whom Jesus brought back to life

Jairus was a synagogue ruler. He asked Jesus to come and put His healing hands on his dying daughter. Then the dreadful news reached Jairus that his daughter had died. But Jesus said, "Do not be afraid; only believe." Jesus then went to her house, took her by the hand, and said, "Talitha cumi." That means "Little girl, I say to you, arise." She was twelve years old.
(See Mark 5:22-43.)

6 Baby hidden in the bulrushes

Moses had an unusual childhood. His mother was a Hebrew captive in Egypt. She was forced to hide him in the bulrushes when he was a baby. All male babies were to be killed at birth. A princess found Moses in the bulrushes. He grew up in Pharaoh's palace. He was given a good education. The name Moses means, "I drew him out of the water."
(See Exodus 2:1-10.)

7 Jesus blessed the children

In New Testament days children were not noticed much. So Jesus shocked people with His care for children. Jesus told the children to come to Him. He said, "Of such is the kingdom of God. Assuredly, I say to you, whoever does not receive the kingdom of God as a little child will by no means enter it." And Jesus took the children in His arms. Then He put His hands on them, and blessed them.
(See Mark 10:13-16.)

8 Boy whom Jesus healed without even meeting

Jesus was back in Cana where He had turned the water into wine. A royal official came up to Him. He begged Him to go to his house in Capernaum. There, his son lay dying. Jesus did something better. He said, "Go your way; your son lives." And without even seeing the boy, Jesus healed him. The boy's fever left at the exact time, the seventh hour, that Jesus said he would get better.
(See John 4:46-54.)

28 WHAT JESUS DID

1 Forgave people's sins

The first thing Jesus said to the paralytic who lay in front of Him was not "I heal you." It was "Son, your sins are forgiven you." The meaning of this was clear to some of the teachers of the law who heard it. Jesus read their thoughts. "Why does this man speak blasphemies like this? Who can forgive sins but God alone?"
(See Mark 2:1-12.)

2 Performed miracles

Just being a miracle worker never got anyone anywhere. Jesus' many miracles were done for a special reason. We learn this through John's comment at the wedding in Cana. Jesus had saved the wedding party. He changed water into wine after their wine ran out. "This beginning of signs Jesus did in Cana of Galilee, and manifested His glory; and His disciples believed in Him."
(See John 2:1-11.)

3 Preached in the open air

The place where Jesus may have given His most famous teaching, the Sermon on the Mount, is now called the Mount of the Beatitudes. Jesus often spoke to crowds of people in the open air. He used examples from the country around them to explain His message.
(See Matthew 5.)

4 Preached in the temple

Jesus was teaching in the temple courts. But He did not please the Jews in the crowd. They could not understand how He could have such knowledge if He had never studied. Jesus told them that His teaching came from God. He did not invent it Himself. Then the people said He had a demon.
(See John 7:14-24.)

5 Made friends with outcasts

You did not have to be poor in Jesus' day to be left out. People loved to hate the tax collectors. They were thought of as traitors. They collected people's hard-earned money for the Romans. Levi, or Matthew, the tax collector left everything and followed Jesus. Then he gave Jesus a party. The Pharisees complained, "Why do You eat and drink with tax collectors and sinners?" Jesus replied, "Those who are well have no need of a physician, but those who are sick. I have not come to call the righteous, but sinners, to repentance."
(See Luke 5:27-32.)

6 Healed the sick

If you were a leper, never again would you feel the touch or hug of a healthy person. A man with leprosy came to Jesus and begged Him on his knees to heal him. He was healed. And he would never forget Jesus' touch. "Then Jesus, moved with compassion, stretched out His hand and touched him."
(See Mark 1:40-45.)

7 Died as Savior

Jesus knew that He would be misunderstood. But He did try to teach His disciples about the meaning of His death. No, He was not going to be just a martyr dying for a good cause. No, He was not going to be just a preacher who ended up on the religious leaders' bad side. Mark 10:45 tells the purpose of His death: "The Son of Man" came "to give His life a ransom for many."

8 Rose from the dead

Jesus tried to explain His death to His disciples. They found it very hard to understand. They thought death would mean the end of Jesus, whom they loved dearly. But Jesus often linked His death with another event. "The Son of Man will be betrayed … and they will condemn Him to death and deliver Him to the Gentiles; and they will mock Him, and scourge Him, and spit on Him, and kill Him. And the third day He will rise again."
(See Mark 10:32-34.)

29 WHAT JESUS SAID

1 Seven "I am's"

Jesus spoke about Himself using the words "I am" in seven ways. Each one tells something about who Jesus was. I am the door. I am the good shepherd. I am the resurrection and the life. I am the way, the truth, and the life. I am the true vine. All seven of these are in John's gospel.
(See John 10:9, 11; 11:25; 14:6; 15:1.)

2 His most famous parable

The most famous parable is probably the Parable of the Prodigal Son. There are the runaway son, the dutiful elder brother, the compassionate father, and the party celebrating the return of the penitent younger son.
(See Luke 15:11-32.)

3 Twenty other parables

Jesus' favorite way of teaching spiritual truth was by parables. Just before the Prodigal Son come the Parable of the Lost Sheep and the Parable of the Lost Coin. The Parable of the Good Samaritan is probably the best-known parable after the Parable of the Prodigal Son. Jesus' parables were stories on two levels. The first level was an interesting story. The second level gave some part of His message. Often it hit home in a most uncomfortable way with His audience.

4 His message to religious leaders

Jesus spoke more severely to the religious leaders of His day than to anyone else. "Woe to you, scribes and Pharisees, hypocrites! For you are like whitewashed tombs which indeed appear beautiful outwardly, but inside are full of dead men's bones and all uncleanness. Even so you also outwardly appear righteous to men, but inside you are full of hypocrisy and lawlessness."
(See Matthew 23:13-36.)

5 What Jesus said to a rich man

Jesus did not tell every person He met the same thing. He did not even tell every rich person He met what He told this rich man: "If you want to be perfect, go, sell what you have and give to the poor, and you will have treasure in heaven; and come, follow Me." (See Matthew 19:16-22.)

6 What Jesus said about a wicked king

Jesus never minced His words. He always praised goodness, truth, and faith in God. He always spoke out against evil. Once some Pharisees came to Jesus and said to Him, "Get out and depart from here, for Herod wants to kill You." Jesus sent a message to Herod through the Pharisees. It began, "Go, tell that fox…." That is not the best way to be popular with those in authority. (See Luke 13:31-35.)

7 Who Jesus said His family is

Jesus taught that Christians make up the largest family imaginable. "'Who is My mother and who are My brothers?' And He stretched out His hand toward His disciples and said, 'Here are My mother and My brothers! For whoever does the will of My Father in heaven is My brother and sister and mother.'" (See Matthew 12:46-50.)

8 First recorded words of Jesus

Jesus returned from fleeing Herod as a baby. He went up to the temple in Jerusalem when He was twelve years old. We know nothing of the years in between. He stayed behind in the temple, talking with the teachers there. What He then told Mary and Joseph are His first recorded words: "Why did you seek Me? Did you not know that I must be about My Father's business?" (See Luke 2:41-52.)

9 Seven "words" from the cross

Jesus said seven things on the cross. The accounts of Jesus' death in the four Gospels make that clear. "Father, forgive them, for they do not know what they do." To His mother, "Woman, behold your son!" and to the disciple, "Behold your mother!" To the penitent thief, "Today you will be with Me in Paradise." "I thirst!" "My God, My God, why have You forsaken Me?" "Father, into Your hands I commit My spirit." And the last "word" (it is a single word in Greek) is a fitting triumphant conclusion to Jesus' work on earth: "It is finished!" (See Luke 23:34; John 19:26-27; Luke 23:43; John 19:28; Matthew 27:46; Luke 23:46; John 19:30.)

30 THE EARLY CHURCH

1 First Christian sermon
The first Christian sermon was given with great fire and passion by Peter. His last line was, "God has made this Jesus, whom you crucified, both Lord and Christ." The result: "Three thousand souls were added to them" that day.
(See Acts 2:14-41.)

2 First sharing of possessions by Christians
Through the centuries, Christians have shared their goods, such as money and property. The first mention of Christians sharing possessions is in Acts 2:44-45. "All who believed were together, and had all things in common, and sold their possessions and goods, and divided them among all, as anyone had need."

3 First imprisonment of Christians
Brave John the Baptist was put in prison because he was faithful to God. Jesus returned to heaven. Then the Holy Spirit came at Pentecost. The first Christians to be put in prison were Peter and John. They taught the people that Jesus had been raised from the dead. This disturbed the priests, the captain of the temple guard, and the Sadducees. They threw Peter and John in prison to "cool off." But "many of those who heard the word believed; and the number of the men came to be about five thousand."
(See Acts 4:1-4.)

4 First Christian martyr
Stephen was full of God's grace and power. He did great miracles and signs among the people. When he was before the council, they "saw his face as the face of an angel." But he was stoned to death. He prayed, "Lord Jesus, receive my spirit." Like Jesus, he prayed for his killers before dying: "Lord, do not charge them with this sin."
(See Acts 6:8–8:2.)

5 Telling a cripple about Jesus

Those who came in the path of the first disciples were told the Christian message. One was a man crippled from birth. He asked Peter and John for money as they entered the temple. Peter said, "Silver and gold I do not have, but what I do have I give you: In the name of Jesus Christ of Nazareth, rise up and walk." (See Acts 3:1-10.)

6 Telling a king about Jesus

The third time that Paul's conversion is recorded is when Paul was explaining the Christian message to King Agrippa. Paul was quite forceful. He did not pull any punches. Paul ended his speech with a question to the king: "King Agrippa, do you believe the prophets? I know that you do believe." The king responded, "You almost persuade me to become a Christian." (See Acts 26:1-32.)

7 Arriving in Rome

For a long time, Paul had wanted to preach the gospel in the center of the known world – Rome. And Paul did go there. He was under arrest to face the emperor. But all he cared about was that he had "two whole years" to preach about the "kingdom of God and … the Lord Jesus Christ." No wonder the last verse of Acts ends on such a high note. (See Acts 28:17-31.)

8 Future is revealed

John was exiled on the island of Patmos. While there, he wrote the book of Revelation. Its first verse says the book is "The Revelation of Jesus Christ, which God gave Him to show His servants – things which must shortly take place." This book has been loved by persecuted Christians. It shows that the history and future of the world are under God's control.